W9-AKD-575

Blue Banner Biography

Vanessa Anne Hudgens

Mary Boone

Mitchell Lane
PUBLISHERS

P.O. Box 196
Hockessin, Delaware 19707
Visit us on the web: www.mitchelllane.com
Comments? email us: mitchelllane@mitchelllane.com

Mitchell Lane PUBLISHERS

Printing   1   2   3   4   5   6   7   8   9

Blue Banner Biographies

Akon	Alan Jackson	Alicia Keys
Allen Iverson	Ashanti	Ashlee Simpson
Ashton Kutcher	Avril Lavigne	Bernie Mac
Beyoncé	Bow Wow	Brett Favre
Britney Spears	Carrie Underwood	Chris Brown
Chris Daughtry	Christina Aguilera	Christopher Paul Curtis
Ciara	Clay Aiken	Condoleezza Rice
Corbin Bleu	Daniel Radcliffe	David Ortiz
Derek Jeter	Eminem	Eve
Fergie (Stacy Ferguson)	50 Cent	Gwen Stefani
Ice Cube	Jamie Foxx	Ja Rule
Jay-Z	Jennifer Lopez	Jessica Simpson
J. K. Rowling	Johnny Depp	JoJo
Justin Berfield	Justin Timberlake	Kanye West
Kate Hudson	Keith Urban	Kelly Clarkson
Kenny Chesney	Lance Armstrong	Lindsay Lohan
Mariah Carey	Mario	Mary J. Blige
Mary-Kate and Ashley Olsen	Michael Jackson	Miguel Tejada
Missy Elliott	Nancy Pelosi	Nelly
Orlando Bloom	P. Diddy	Paris Hilton
Peyton Manning	Queen Latifah	Rihanna
Ron Howard	Rudy Giuliani	Sally Field
Sean Kingston	Selena	Shakira
Shirley Temple	Soulja Boy Tell 'Em	Taylor Swift
Timbaland	Tim McGraw	Toby Keith
Usher	**Vanessa Anne Hudgens**	Zac Efron

Library of Congress Cataloging-in-Publication Data
Boone, Mary, 1963–
    Vanessa Anne Hudgens / by Mary Boone.
        p. cm. — (Blue banner biographies)
    Includes bibliographical references and index.
    ISBN 978-1-58415-672-7 (library bound)
    1. Hudgens, Vanessa, 1988– —Juvenile literature. 2. Actors—United States—Biography—Juvenile literature. 3. Singers—United States—Biography—Juvenile literature. I. Title.
    PN2287.H737B66 2009
    791.4302'8092—dc22
    [B]
                                                                                2008013229

ABOUT THE AUTHOR: Mary Boone has written a dozen books for young adults, including biographies about Corbin Bleu, Akon, and 50 Cent for Mitchell Lane Publishers. She also has written for magazines including *People, Teen People, Mary-Kate and Ashley,* and *Entertainment Weekly.* Boone lives in Tacoma, Washington. When she's not writing she enjoys running, swimming, and being outdoors with her husband, Mitch, and their two children, Eve and Eli.

PUBLISHER'S NOTE: The following story has been thoroughly researched, and to the best of our knowledge represents a true story. While every possible effort has been made to ensure accuracy, the publisher will not assume liability for damages caused by inaccuracies in the data and makes no warranty on the accuracy of the information contained herein. This story has not been authorized or endorsed by Vanessa Anne Hudgens.

Blue Banner Biography

Thanks in large part to her role as Gabriella in High School Musical,
Vanessa Anne Hudgens has been propelled to stardom. She landed a
record deal, and scores of new movie offers began rolling in.

A Young Performer

Vanessa Anne Hudgens didn't even tell her parents about her first theatrical role.

"I guess it never crossed my mind to tell them," she told *The [Philippine] Inquirer.*

The oversight is probably understandable, considering Hudgens was just a toddler at the time. She had been cast in her school's Christmas pageant and was more excited about her prop than the fame that lay ahead.

"I told my mom I needed a baby doll," she said. "So, she went out and bought me a baby doll, which was a huge thing. I always had hand-me-downs, so I was excited to have my new doll."

Doll in hand, she asked her parents to take her to school one evening. The family was living in Oregon, and a snowstorm almost kept them home. Good thing they shoveled the driveway, because they got to school just in time for the show.

"My parents got to see me singing 'Away in a Manger.' I was holding little baby Jesus and I was Mother Mary," she recalled. "Since then, I have always loved acting, singing and dancing. I would dance around my house when I was three years old, choreographing my own dances to [C+C Music Factory's] 'Everybody Dance Now.' "

Those watching Hudgens' preschool performance probably had no idea she'd become the sensation she is today, starring in Disney's popular *High School Musical* movies and becoming a multiplatinum recording artist before she turned twenty.

Born on December 14, 1988, in Salinas, California, Hudgens' talents were obvious almost from the beginning. Dance, piano, and vocal lessons helped polish her skills and prepared her for roles in local productions of *Carousel*, *The Wizard of Oz*, and *Cinderella*.

Her big break came when a friend couldn't make it to an audition for a television commercial. She asked Hudgens to go in her place.

> *Casting directors were drawn to Vanessa's quiet charm and dark, expressive eyes.*

"Fortunately, I booked it," she told *The Inquirer*. "I was doing tons of community theater at the time, so I was already used to doing musicals and stuff. One thing led to another. I did the commercial and then another one."

That taste of success convinced Greg and Gina Hudgens to move to Los Angeles so that their daughter could pursue a full-time acting career. Their sacrifice paid off. Casting directors were drawn to Vanessa's quiet charm and dark, expressive eyes. She quickly built her acting resume with

Vanessa celebrates Father's Day with her dad, Greg Hudgens, at the launch of Techno Source's new electronic game, Rubik's Revolution, in 2007. Family support has made a huge difference in Vanessa Hudgens' career.

Vanessa isn't the only Hudgens with star power: Little sister Stella models and has appeared in television series including Deeply Irresponsible, According to Jim, *and* American Family.

guest roles on television shows including Nickelodeon's *The Brothers Garcia* and CBS's *Still Standing*.

She made her feature film debut in 2003's *Thirteen*. The critically acclaimed film offers a brutal look at the world of a young teen trying to fit in with a fast group of seventh-graders in Los Angeles. Hudgens' role was small, but it allowed her a chance to share screen time with big names, including Oscar-winner Holly Hunter and Golden Globe–nominee Evan Rachel Wood. It also got her foot in the door in Hollywood.

Hudgens' next feature film was *Thunderbirds*, a family-friendly flick about a high-tech secret force employed by the government. The 2004 live-action movie costarred Bill Paxton. Even though the movie fell flat at the box office, Hudgens used the experience to build both her connections and her experience.

She went on to land guest roles in sitcoms including *Quintuplets* and *The Suite Life of Zack and Cody*. Hudgens was balancing schoolwork, acting classes, and auditions when she first read the script for a Disney made-for-TV movie called *High School Musical*. She fell in love with the storyline and knew she wanted to be part of it.

Hudgens was balancing schoolwork, acting classes, and auditions when she first read the script for a Disney made-for-TV movie . . .

"I was a struggling actor looking for a job and I loved musicals," she told *Tampa Bay Online*. "I went in there to audition and gave it my best and was fortunate to get it. I loved the project."

Soren Fulton and Vanessa Hudgens arrive at the 2004 premiere of their movie Thunderbirds. *The film, based on a 1960s television series by the same name, performed poorly at the box office.*

And, thanks to that project, Vanessa Anne Hudgens has gone from obscurity to superstardom.

From Bit Parts to Big Time

No one could have suspected *High School Musical* would be the red-hot commodity it has become. More than 7.7 million viewers watched *High School Musical*'s premiere on January 20, 2006. The made-for-TV movie was the number one movie of the month on all basic cable networks. The film, which cost $4.2 million to make, earned nearly $1 billion for the Disney Channel.

HSM became a hit in more than 100 countries. It has spawned books, toys, video games, clothing, dolls, posters, a concert tour, stage versions, and a nationally touring ice show.

In the film, Hudgens portrays Gabriella Montez. Gabriella is a quiet but brainy transfer student who finds herself drawn to East High's star athlete and resident hunk, Troy Bolton (played by Zac Efron). Together they try out for the school musical and break free from their cliques.

Hudgens told InsideBayArea.com that she's not so different from her on-screen persona. "I was born in Salinas, [California,] but I grew up all over the country. I lived in small towns, in San Diego, gosh, a lot of places. I was totally shy growing up and, like Gabriella, never lived in one place for too long, so I related to her."

And, like their characters Gabriella and Troy, Hudgens and costar Efron fell in love during the making of the movie. It was a relationship they tried to keep secret—but that wasn't really possible.

Hudgens quickly learned that nothing in her life was private anymore. Photographers began following her to the mall, to coffee shops, and even to the gym. While she and Efron were vacationing in Hawaii, photographers snapped pictures of them snuggling on the beach. Soon the photos were printed in magazines and online. Their once-secret relationship had become public, and the media even began referring to the couple as "Zanessa"—a combination of their first names.

Suddenly cast as a role model for tweens and teens, Hudgens relished the opportunity to set a good example for young fans.

While some young starlets actually like the attention, Hudgens tried to avoid it. "I became an actress and started singing and dancing because I truly loved it," she told Australia's *Daily Telegraph*. "I did not want to be a celebrity. . . . I think fame is just something that comes along when you are in something that is such a success."

Suddenly cast as a role model for tweens and teens, Hudgens relished the opportunity to set a good example for young fans. Magazines ran article after article about her "squeaky clean image."

That's why it came as a shock when nude photos of the actress hit the Internet in September 2007. The photos, which reportedly had been taken several years earlier, were emailed to a friend when Hudgens had been a virtual unknown. The scandal had film industry insiders speculating that Disney, which prides itself on its wholesome image, would cut ties with Hudgens.

The success of High School Musical *made instant stars of its six lead actors, left to right standing: Vanessa Hudgens, Monique Coleman, and Ashley Tisdale; left to right kneeling: Corbin Bleu, Lucas Grabeel, and Zac Efron.*

After spending several days in seclusion, Hudgens released a statement about the incident: "I want to apologize to my fans, whose support and trust means the world to me. I am embarrassed over this situation and regret having ever taken these photos. I am thankful for the support of my family and friends."

The fact that Hudgens took responsibility for her actions seemed to sit well with Disney executives. The studio stood by the young starlet, saying it had no plans to recast the role of Gabriella Montez. Disney's official statement went on to say: "Vanessa has apologized for what was obviously a lapse in judgment. It is a personal matter and it is unfortunate that this has become public."

> *The fact that Hudgens took responsibility for her actions seemed to sit well with Disney executives.*

Hudgens rebounded from the public embarrassment and hopes to keep it in her past. "Truthfully, I don't like talking about it," she told *Seventeen* magazine. "It was very traumatic and I'm extremely upset it happened. I hope all my fans can learn from my mistake and make smart decisions."

The incident also taught her that, while fame may be fleeting, family support is always important. "I wouldn't have been able to get through it if it wasn't for my family, friends and fans who supported me along the way," she told *Seventeen*. "My parents are very supportive of me. And they know I'm a teenager and, yes, kids do stupid things sometimes."

High School: Parts 2 and 3

*H*igh School Musical was such a huge hit that studio executives wasted no time planning a sequel. It was clear that fans wanted to see more of Troy, Gabriella, and the gang.

High School Musical 2 caught up with the East High students on their last day of school and followed them to their summer jobs at a posh country club—where Ashley Tisdale's and Lucas Grabeel's characters, Sharpay and Ryan, are members. Hudgens' character, Gabriella, works as a lifeguard at the club, while Troy (Efron) works in the golf shop, Chad (Corbin Bleu) toils in the kitchen, and Taylor (Monique Coleman) works in the activities office. As the characters encounter their own on-the-job challenges, they face off over the country club's annual midsummer night's musical production.

Fans drawn to Troy and Gabriella's budding romance weren't disappointed. *HSM2* definitely fans the flame of on-screen love.

"I wish I could put my finger on what makes our chemistry work on-screen," Efron told the *Inquirer*. "But I

Efron and Hudgens pose with the 2006 Emmy Awards that High School Musical *earned. It won for Outstanding Children's Program and Outstanding Choreography.*

can tell you that [Hudgens is] easy to talk to, very kind, sweet and she has a great sense of humor. When you combine that with an amazing voice and beauty, you're going to have a star. She's amazing to work with."

Cast and crew returned to Utah to film *High School Musical 2*. Because of actors' conflicting schedules, they had less than three weeks to learn and rehearse ten original numbers and less than a month to shoot.

The movie, which was expected to do well, did not disappoint. When it debuted on August 17, 2007, *High School Musical 2* had an audience of more than 17.2 million viewers, making it the highest-rated basic cable broadcast of all time. The movie easily beat out the previous record-holder, the September 2006 debut of *Monday Night Football* on ESPN, which drew 16 million viewers. A couple of weeks after the debut, Disney began airing a special dance-along version of *High School Musical 2*. Hudgens, Efron, and company hosted the show and instructed viewers on how to imitate their dances.

> **When it debuted on August 17, 2007, High School Musical 2 had an audience of more than 17.2 million viewers.**

As if all that weren't enough, the first week of sales for the sound track CD of *High School Musical 2* saw 615,000 copies move off the shelves, making it the second-hottest CD of the year, just behind the debut of Linkin Park's *Minutes to Midnight,* which sold 623,000 copies during its debut week.

Disney Channel Worldwide Entertainment President Gary Marsh told News.com.au that the *High School Musical* phenomenon "touched people in ways that made them want to embrace it as part of their lives."

"Maybe the world is so filled with fear right now that people were ready for an uplifting, magical experience," he said.

If that's what fans want, Disney is more than happy to deliver. The third installment in the *High School Musical* series was set for release in movie theaters in October 2008. The film follows Gabriella, Troy, and friends as they get ready for prom and graduation, the whole time struggling with the idea of being separated from one another as college approaches.

"I am so excited," Hudgens told People magazine. "To do a third one for the big screen, I can't begin to think how much fun we'll have."

"I am so excited," Hudgens told *People* magazine when asked about returning for *HSM3*. "To do a third one for the big screen, I can't begin to think how much fun we'll have."

Are there hopes for an *HSM4*? Director Kenny Ortega told *US Weekly*, "I have a feeling [*HSM3*] will be the end for the current stars." But he hinted there would be more installments of *High School Musical* when he said, "This franchise may move to another generation."

Hitting the High Notes

*H*igh School Musical owes much of its success to its catchy choreography and sassy songs. Within days of its initial airing, fans were singing along to the songs and copying the cast's dance steps. Even industry executives were shocked when the sound track from the first *High School Musical* movie became the number one album of 2006, thanks in large part to songs like "Breaking Free" and "When There Was Me and You" — on both of which Hudgens sings lead vocals. By 2008, the sound track had sold more than 4 million copies, outpacing albums by such popular artists as Rascal Flatts, Carrie Underwood, and Justin Timberlake.

The movie's popularity led to a 40-city tour called High School Musical: The Concert. The tour sold out 42 arenas across North America. After a short break to film *High School Musical 2,* the tour continued through Spring 2007 in Europe, Australia, and Latin America. Efron was the only original cast member who did not go on the road (he was filming the movie *Hairspray*). That left singer Drew Seeley (who sang Troy's parts in the original *High School Musical*) to fill in for him on the tour.

"It's like being in another world," Hudgens told InsideBayArea.com. "We go to countries where they don't even speak the same language and they are singing our songs."

High School Musical *showcased Hudgens' acting and vocal talents. Music studio executives, who liked her sound and marketability, courted the young songstress. She decided to release her debut album, V, on the Hollywood Records label.*

In September 2006, Hudgens proved she's more than just an ensemble player. She signed with Hollywood Records and released her debut album, *V*. It was a huge step for someone who always considered herself more of an actor than a singer.

"Singing was something I was good at, but never really thought of pursuing," she told the *Inquirer*. After *High School Musical*, though, she was approached by several studios.

"Finally, I picked Hollywood Records and made my album, *V*. It was a learning experience being in the studio and finding out what kind of music suits my voice best. I tried different kinds of music. I did pop, R&B and rock. I threw it all together and had this collection of different music which is why I call it *V*. The *V* is not only for *Vanessa* but for *variety* because there's a different mixture of music there."

Her first single, "Come Back to Me," was hugely successful. Her song "Let's Dance" has been used in commercials for both *Desperate Housewives* and *Dancing with the Stars*.

Elysa Gardner of *People* magazine wrote in her review of the album that Hudgens' vocals "suggest a baby J.Lo [Jennifer Lopez]." She said the CD was a great showcase for Hudgens, and that the singles combined to create "a tasty assortment of ear candy."

> *Hudgens proved she's more than just an ensemble player. She signed with Hollywood Records and released her debut album, V.*

Even before the *HSM* tour, Hudgens went on the road with The Cheetah Girls. She opened sixteen shows on the girl group's The Party's Just Begun tour. It was Hudgens' first taste of the live concert scene.

"Touring is tough," she told ShowBuzz.com. "You're in a haze because you really don't know where you are half the time. You're in a hotel room one moment and the next thing you know, you're onstage, performing for 60,000 people, then you're back on an airplane. It's very hectic."

It's a pace Hudgens may have to learn to embrace. When her second album was released in summer 2008, the songbird was destined to go on the road again to promote it.

Hudgens says the project, titled *Identified*, has a more grown-up sound than her debut effort.

> *Even before the HSM tour, Hudgens went on the road with The Cheetah Girls. She opened sixteen shows on the girl group's The Party's Just Begun tour.*

"It really reflects who I am," she told *Seventeen*. "It's not at all what people are expecting. I get bored easily, so I really wanted to reinvent myself and do something different — what I wanted to do. And this time around it's a lot jazzier, and a lot more hip-hop and R&B."

Tracks on the album include "Whisper," "It Feels Right," and "I Will," a song written by former Disney star Hilary Duff.

"I feel like I'm creating my own genre," she said. "It's completely different from what people have heard from me."

Life After High School

*H*udgens dreams of someday playing the role of Maria in a production of *West Side Story*. Beyond that, she told *Variety*, "I don't really have a specific career plan. I'd just love to do movies in every genre."

She may get that chance.

The first post–*High School Musical* opportunity Hudgens seized was a role in the feature film *Will*. The movie, which tells the story of a high school outcast's bond with a popular girl as they assemble a rock band for their school's battle-of-the-bands competition, also stars Lisa Kudrow (*Friends; P.S., I Love You*) and Scott Porter (*Friday Night Lights, Prom Night*). Hudgens would play Sam, a fifteen-year-old who used to stutter.

With *Will* set for release in early 2009, Hudgens was busy reading scripts and considering her options among many film, television, music, and business proposals. College, too, may be in her future—but not yet.

"Education is really important," she told the *Inquirer* in fall 2007. "It is something that will be with you forever. I definitely want to get a college education when the time is

Actor Gaelan Connell plays the title character in the 2009 movie Will, *and Hudgens plays the part of Sam. Alyson Michalka, of Aly and AJ fame, would also star.*

right. Right now, the opportunities that I have are too amazing to pass up."

An admitted fashion fanatic (she has three closets devoted solely to shoes), Hudgens has already done promotional work for Red by Marc Ecko apparel and footwear and Neutrogena beauty products. Designing her own brand of clothing or accessories is a definite possibility. "Down the line, I also want to have my own clothing line," she told *Variety*.

She'd also like to travel to her mother's home country, the Philippines. "I am so proud of my heritage," she told that country's newspaper, the *Inquirer*. "I love being a Filipina. There aren't very many Filipino girls in the industry, so being able to stand up and be that girl makes me proud. My mother is so proud; she grew up in Manila. . . . I'd love to make it over there someday. Unfortunately, I have not had a chance to visit."

With so many possibilities ahead of her, Hudgens works hard not to forget about the here and now. She devotes her time and energy to a number of charities. One of her favorites is Best Buddies International, a Miami-based program that provides employment opportunities for and one-on-one friendships to people with mental disabilities.

"It's really neat to reach out to people who are fans, too," she told ShowBizSpy.com. "Just to be able to be a part of their lives is really neat."

> She'd also like to travel to her mother's home country, the Philippines. "I am so proud of my heritage," she said.

Hudgens poses with a fan at the 2007 Best Buddies International Lucky Strike Lanes fund-raiser in Hollywood. The charity provides support for people with mental disabilities.

Hudgens and High School Musical *costar Ashley Tisdale pose with fans at A Time for Heroes, a Disney-sponsored event to benefit the Elizabeth Glaser Pediatric AIDS Foundation. Reaching out to fans and supporting worthwhile causes is important to these stars.*

Unlike many young stars, Hudgens prefers watching movies with friends to nights on the town. She's seen fame have disastrous effects on the lives of some of her peers and predecessors.

"People become jaded and infatuated with Hollywood," she told *People.* "I think it happens to a lot of celebrities and it messes with their heads."

The young performer is also determined to continue refining her talents so that she might someday disprove those who think she's just another pretty face. "I am talented," she told *Seventeen*. "I think pretty girls in general get a lot of crap in the business because it's all, 'You're too pretty for that part—we need someone who's grittier.' But, somewhere down the line, I'm going to prove everybody wrong."

> *Other than shopping more, Hudgens says she's the same girl she was before the chart-topping hits and record-setting movies.*

Other than shopping more, Hudgens says she's the same girl she was before the chart-topping hits and record-setting movies. "I'm still the same person and I do still hang out with the same friends," she told *Discovery Girls* magazine. "I grew up in a small town and living in Hollywood can change the way you look at things, the way you dress, and even the way you act. What keeps me grounded is seeing other people change and knowing how much I hate it. That makes me never want to change."

Hudgens says her album Identified *is "fun, and it's funky, and it's fresh."*

1988 Vanessa Anne Hudgens is born December 14 in Salinas, California, to Greg Hudgens and Gina Guangco Hudgens.

1995 Vanessa's sister Stella is born.

2002 Vanessa makes her TV debut on an episode of CBS's *Still Standing*.

2003 She makes her feature film debut as Noel in *Thirteen*.

2004 She appears as Tintin in the film *Thunderbirds*.

2005 She is cast as Gabriella Montez in *High School Musical*.

2006 *High School Musical* airs January 20. It becomes Disney Channel's most successful movie at the time, with 7.7 million viewers for its first U.S. broadcast. She participates in the Disney Channel Games. Her first album, *V*, is released by Hollywood Records in September, debuting at number 24 on the Billboard Hot 200.

2007 With estimated earnings of $2 million, Hudgens ranks number 7 on *Forbes* magazine's list of top-earning stars under 21. *High School Musical 2* premieres August 17 to 17.2 million viewers, making it the most-watched event ever broadcast on basic cable. Hudgens appears in commercials for Blockbuster and Old Navy, and becomes the new face of Neutrogena. She becomes the subject of a nude photo scandal. *USA Today* ranks Hudgens No. 43 on its Hot 50 Celebrity Heat Index.

2008 She begins filming *High School Musical 3: Senior Year*. She is cast in the coming-of-age movie *Will*. Her second album, *Identified*, is released.

DISCOGRAPHY

2008 *Identified*
2006 *V*

Sound Track Contributions/Compilations
2007 *High School Musical 2 Soundtrack*
2006 *Girl Next* (2 volumes)
High School Musical Soundtrack

FILMOGRAPHY

Theater Releases
2009 *Will*
2008 *High School Musical 3:*
        Senior Year
2004 *Thunderbirds*
2003 *Thirteen*

Television
2007 *High School Musical 2*
2006 *High School Musical*
        Guest role on *Drake & Josh*
        Guest role on *Suite Life of*
        Zack and Cody
2005 Guest role on *Quintuplets*
2003 Guest role on *The Brothers*
        Garcia
2002 Guest role on *Still Standing*

FURTHER READING

Books

Boone, Mary. *Corbin Bleu*. Hockessin, Delaware: Mitchell Lane Publishers, 2009.

Norwich, Grace. *Vanessa Hudgens: Breaking Free: An Unauthorized Biography.* New York: Price Stern Sloan, 2007.

Tracy, Kathleen. *Zac Efron*. Hockessin, Delaware: Mitchell Lane Publishers, 2008.

Works Consulted

Belcher, Walt. "Zanessa Says." *Tampa Bay Online*, August 16, 2007, http://www.tbo.com/life/MGBMYD26E5F.html.

Bianco, Robert. " 'High School Musical' Sequel Holds On to Note of Innocence." *USA Today*, August 16, 2007.

Blair, Iain. " 'High School' Actress Copes with Pressure." *Variety*, October 4, 2007.

Campbell, Janis. "Q&A with Vanessa Hudgens: 'HSM' Star Talks School, Work and Play." *Detroit Free Press*, August 14, 2007.

"Celebrity Central: Vanessa Hudgens." *People*, www.people.com.

Critchell, Samantha. " 'High School Musical 2' Stars Have Their Own High Style." The Associated Press, August 21, 2007.

Downie, Stephen. "*High School Musical*'s Vanessa Hudgens Laments on Fame," News.com.au. November 28, 2007, http://www.news.com.au/entertainment/story/0,23663,22836271-5007183,00.html.

"Hudgens Clicked with Efron Early On." CBS Interactive Inc.'s *The Showbuzz*, August 17, 2007, http://www.showbuzz.cbsnews.com/stories/2007/08/17/tv/main3178493.shtml.

Keveney, Bill. " 'Musical' Stars Over the Moon About Success." *USA Today*, August 16, 2007. http://www.usatoday.com/life/television/news/2007-08-16-HSM2-chart_N.htm

Kinon, Cristina. "HSM2 Kicks Off Marketing Sell-ebration." *[New York] Daily News*, August 17, 2007.

———. "Ashley Tisdale, Vanessa Hudgens Friends since 'High School.' " *[New York] Daily News*, August 21, 2007.

"L.A. Judge Says Hudgens Suit Can Go Ahead." *The Associated Press*, December 6, 2007.

Martinez, Jennifer. "Daily Entertainment Break: Vanessa Hudgens Tells All about 'HSM 3.' " *The [San Jose, Calif.,] Mercury News*, November 30, 2007.

Miller, Gerri. "The Stars of 'High School Musical 2' Hit the High Notes." http://www.hollywood.com/feature/High_School_Musical_2_Zac_Efron_Ashley_Tisdale_Vanessa_Hudgens/4693445

Nepales, Ruben V. "Vanessa Hudgens: 'I Love Being a Filipina.' " *[Philippines] Inquirer*, August 9, 2007, http://showbizandstyle.inquirer.net/entertainment/entertainment/view_article.php?article_id=81617

Nudd, Tim. "Vanessa Hudgens: I Didn't Want to Be a Celebrity." *People*, November 28, 2007, http://www.people.com/people/article/0,,20162998,00.html

Silverman, Stephen M. "No Surprise: 'High School Musical 2' Is a Massive Hit." *People*, August 20, 2007. http://www.people.com/people/article/0,,20052472,00.html

Tyers, Alan. "Tween Star Is Squeaky-Clean." *The [London] Sun*, August 31, 2007. http://www.thesun.co.uk/sol/homepage/showbiz/tv/article267076.ece

"Vanessa Hudgens 'Embarrassed,' Apologizes for Nude Photo." *People*, September 7, 2007. http://www.people.com/people/article/0,,20055380,00.html

"Who's the Hottest of Them All?" *USA Today*, December 24, 2007.

Young, Susan. "Back to 'School': Kenny Ortega, Zac Efron, Vanessa Hudgens and the Gang Are Back for 'High School Musical 2'." *Oakland Tribune*, August 14, 2007, http://findarticles.com/p/articles/mi_qn4176/is_20070814/ai_n19468481

On the Internet
Vannessa Anne Hudgens
http://www.vanessaannehudgens.net/
http://hollywoodrecords.go.com/vanessahudgens

INDEX

Photo Credits: Cover—Alexander Tamargo/Getty Images; p. 4—Vera Anderson/WireImage/Getty Images; p. 7—Gary Gershof/WireImage for Ruth C. Schwartz and Co., Inc./Getty Images; pp. 8, 26—Jordan Strauss/WireImage/Getty Images; p. 10—Mike Marsland/WireImage/Getty Images; p. 13—FilmMagic/Getty Images; p. 16—John Sciulli/WireImage/Getty Images; p. 16—Tim Mosenfelder/Getty Images; p. 24—James Devaney/WireImage/Getty Images; p. 27—Lester Cohen/WireImage for Elizabeth Glaser Pediatric AIDS/Getty Images.